I0481842

Be A Billion Dollar Entrepreneurial Leader!

Colin Emerson

Be A Billion Dollar Entrepreneurial Leader!

Enquiries should be addressed to:
Colin Emerson
colin@InaSenseGroup.com

ISBN 978-1723273346

Created in Australia by
In A Sense Group
www.InaSenseGroup.com

Printed by
CreateSpace,
Charleston SC

Dedicated to:

To all everyone who has ever believed in a dream and pursued it.
To anyone who has a dream and is poised to make it happen.
and
To everyone who ever believed in those that had a dream.

Without dreamers, there is no magic.

"Men (*and women*) make history and not the other way around. In periods where there is no leadership, society stands still. Progress occurs when courageous, skilful leaders seize the opportunity to change things for the better."

Harry S. Truman
1884 – 1972
33rd President of the United States:
1945 to 1953

Took office in April 1945 following the death of Franklin D Roosevelt. Within days of taking office, he was required to make the fateful decision to use an atomic bomb in a theatre of war. Following WWII, he implemented the Marshall Plan to rebuild Western Europe, established NATO and was a founding signatory of the United Nations.

"A ship in port is safe; but that is not what ships are built for. Sail out to sea and do new things"

Admiral "Amazing" Grace Hopper
1906 – 1992
Admiral, United States Navy

A woman who literally changed the world & should be an inspiration to everyone. If you have ever used a computer or mobile device, then you have been touched by the work of "Amazing Grace", as she became known. She earned her PhD in mathematics in 1931. But it was her work in computer languages after WWII that led to a most significant event in computer programming, one that makes ordinary computers into the multi-talented functioning machines they are today. She created the 'Compiler'. This is a program that transforms source code of one computer language into another, usually less complex, language. Steve Jobs & Bill Gates owe a lot of their success to this lady. Read her story in: *'Grace Hopper and the Invention of the Information Age'*
by Kurt W. Beyer

-The Billion Dollar Entrepreneurial Leader-

Imagine. You've just arrived in a major city you've only ever visited twice before and both of those time were 30 years previous and both were only overnight stays.

It's early evening and you're set up in a hotel room that will be home for the next 6 weeks while you find somewhere more permanent to live.

You've just taken on a role you have never done before in a profession to which you are relatively new. You know absolutely nobody who lives in the city.

Next morning you walk to a building you have never seen and meet seven people, five who you have never met and two you met on one day three weeks ago. Only three of the other people know each other.

Effectively, we're all meeting each other for the very first time, in an office we have never seen before to work with a company that only half of us have worked for before this day.

This is day one of a whole new business in a city already dominated by five well-established and market-dominant brands.

As a State Manager, it's your job to bring your team together and along with the State Credit Manager and their team, take on five established, major banks.... and anyone else who wants to take you on.... and become successful.

You have no radio or TV advertising budget. You don't make a dint in any brand awareness surveys. After all, the company, as a whole, had only received a banking licence three months ago. It's that new a bank.

Imagine then how it felt, in just under three years, when we celebrated the milestone of achieving a billion dollars in growth, in achieving a 14% market-share across all banking products and settling 25% of all housing loans month-on-month in the state; of having a brand awareness of around 80% in a city that, three years previous, didn't even know you existed.

Imagine, out of a national sales force of nearly 80, the team you have assembled and worked with are placed 1st, 3rd, 4th, 5th, 7th, 8th and 10th, with the one internal sales member of the team rated 2nd nationally. All achieved in what was the second smallest market in the country.

Imagine all of that and you begin to understand the journey I took in becoming a Billion Dollar Leader. Imagine all of that and you begin to understand the calibre of the people I was blessed to bring together and work with.

But that understanding only covers the success side of the story. Behind that success are many smaller stories, some successful, some not so. It doesn't tell you how we did all that we did and what it takes to start with very little and turn it into a billion dollars.

You have to think differently. You have to act differently. You have to be entrepreneurial in what you do and how you do it.

That's what this book is about. To give you an insight into what it takes for you to become a Billion Dollar Entrepreneurial Leader in your own right.

The fact is, it can be done. The fact is, it's not easy. The fact is, it will take an extraordinary level of idea creation way beyond what most people are willing to do. But that's what makes a Billion Dollar Entrepreneurial Leader so extra-ordinary.

Colin Emerson
July 2018

"The biggest risk is not taking any risk… In a world that's changing really quickly, the only strategy that is guaranteed to fail is not taking risks"

Mark Zuckerberg
1984 – Current
Co-founder, CEO and Chairman of Facebook

Mark Zuckerberg (along with roommates Eduardo Saverin, Andrew McCollum, Dustin Moskovitz, and Chris Hughes launched) Facebook from his dormitory room on February 4, 2004, while attending Harvard University. In June 2016, he was named by Business Insider as one of the "Top 10 Business Visionaries Creating Value for the World" along with Elon Musk and Sal Khan, when he and his wife "pledged to give away 99% of their wealth"; estimated at over $52 billion.

- Table of Contents -

"Every day you may make progress. Every step may be fruitful. Yet there will stretch out before you an ever-lengthening, ever-ascending, ever-improving path. You know you will never get to the end of the journey. But this, so far from discouraging, only adds to the joy and glory of the climb. Success is not final, failure is not fatal, it is the courage to continue that counts. This is the lesson: never give in, never give in, never, never, never, never — in nothing, great or small, large or petty — never give in."

Sir Winston Churchill
1874 – 1965
Prime Minister of United Kingdom:
1940 – 1945 & 1951 - 1955

Born into an aristocratic family, Winston Churchill would lead the British nation through the darkest hours of WWII to victory in 1945. He was often considered somewhat of a noisy nuisance, being one of the few to speak out against Nazism in the 1930s, with his predictions of war and later, to declare that the 'Iron Curtain' of Communism would descend upon Europe with the close of the war. His views, at the time were considered as alarmist, but both would be proven correct. Admired, controversial, Nobel Prize winner (literature), social reformer and Imperialist, he is still considered as one of the most influential and significant leaders of the 20th Century.

"The best way to not feel hopeless is to get up and do something. Don't wait for good things to happen to you. If you go out and make some good things happen, you will fill the world with hope, you will fill yourself with hope"

Barack Obama
1961 – current
44th President of the United States:
2009 – 2017

Civil rights attorney and professor of constitutional law at the University of Chicago Law School. His main reforms as President were the Patient Protection and Affordable Care Act and the Dodd–Frank Wall Street Reform and Consumer Protection Act.

Chapter 1

– Commit To Act! –

Your entrepreneurial journey starts with a commitment to act.

You can have the greatest idea in history. But without a commitment to act, it will only ever be an idea. You can have the dream to live a life that brings the best to you and those you love, a dream to change lives and the world or a dream to be free to be the very best you can be.

But without a commitment to act, it will only ever remain a dream.

In the Disney movie, Pinocchio (1940), Jiminy Cricket sang, "When you wish upon a star...your dreams come true". Not one to argue with the brilliance of Walt Disney (1901 – 1966), nor downplaying the absolute importance of having a dream, but wishing and hoping and wanting a dream to come true is a waste _IF_ it is not matched by the commitment to act.

Commit to act and you are committing to making your entrepreneurial dream a reality.

In becoming a Billion-Dollar Leader, I had to first commit to stepping out into a situation I had no idea would work, or not. I committed to doing everything I could to make it happen. I committed to finding the people who could help make it happen.

Commit! Commit! Commit!

Commit implies a pledge or an obligation. It's not half-hearted. It's a full-on, 100% binding promise to do something beyond the normal.

You can play safe and not commit, but is that really what you want to be remembered for?

"If your actions inspire others to dream more, learn more, do more and become more, you are a leader."

John Quincy Adams
1767 – 1848
6th President of the United States:
1825 – 1829

John Quincy Adams was one of America's great Secretaries of State and well-respected Diplomat, arranging for the occupation of the Oregon country with England, obtaining from Spain the cession of the Floridas, and formulating, with President Monroe, the Monroe Doctrine; declaring that America would "not to be considered as subjects for future colonization by any European powers". On the quirky side, shortly after entering the White House he installed a billiards table and would often swim naked in the early mornings in the Potomac river. In his later years as the U.S. Representative from Massachusetts, upon leaving the White House, he became a leading opponent of Slavery in the USA.

But note the second part of the statement. Commit to act.

It takes courage to act when you not absolutely certain of the results. But being an entrepreneur is not about certainty. It's about taking a calculated risk – to challenge the world to prove you wrong in the pursuit of your dream.

Action is about doing. It's about finding out what you can do, should do and must do – and then doing it as best as you can – or finding those that can if you can't.

It's constantly assessing the outcomes of your decisions and being flexible enough to adapt and move forward, even when things don't quite turn out as you planned.

I didn't have time to wait around while having useless meetings and thinking about 5-year action-plans and having talk-fests about possibilities. Discussions were had, plans were made and initial short-term targets set, but within days, not months.

There was no time to wait until things were perfect; it was out there, talking to people who could help generate business, organising events and getting to know those I needed to know. The longer-term plans could wait until I knew more about the world I was now immerged in.

Entrepreneurs can't wait until everything is safe until they act. They gather as much information they can as quickly as they can and then act to do what they can – while they make their plans for the next phase of growth.

They are builders. They are adapters. They are cautionary risk takers, gathering what they need to in order to make the next quick strike. They act while most people are still thinking about it.

"Whether you think you can or you think you can't, you're right"

Henry Ford

1863 – 1947

Founder of the Ford Motor Company

His implementation of the assembly line technique of mass production led the way in producing affordable motor vehicles and transformed much of the way in which goods were, and still are, produced. 15,007,034 Model 'T' Fords were built between 1908 and 1927, when production of the 'T' ceased.

An entrepreneur believes unreservedly in the things they want to achieve. They have faith that all will work out – and if it doesn't, they have faith that they will find an answer to any problem they face.

They'll ask the question, "why?". And once they know their why, they'll jump in with a wholehearted, "why not?". They are not naive and stupidly blasé, but, are willingly optimistic in their ability to adapt to any erroneous position that decision may bring, just as much as they have faith that it will work and there will be benefits from their decision.

The trouble is, most entrepreneurs have that belief long before their people do. That leaves their people often wondering who the hell is leading them? Who is this nutter? Can't blame them for that! Entrepreneurs often implement ideas way before their people are prepared for them.

The key is gathering those around you who can understand what you are trying to do. Who can see your vision. Who are willing to accept the temporary insanity of you, their leader, while they grow to greater understanding and acceptance of where your insanity and vision is taking them.

They need to understand that every decision you make is thought out and is never meant to harm, only grow.

But it takes time for trust to become a two-way street.

Bring your people, even third and fourth party suppliers and contractors, into your circle of confidence. Let them become a visionary with you. You never know what left-field ideas their insanity will come up with once you set them free to believe also.

And those ideas may just be the very ones that will become your own billion-dollar story.

"There is a difference between being a leader and being a boss. Both are based on authority. A boss demands blind obedience; a leader earns his authority through understanding and trust"

Klaus Balkenhol

1939 – current

German and Olympic Equestrian Champion

Won Gold in team dressage at the 1992 Olympics in Barcelona and Gold at the 1996 Atlanta Olympics.

Chapter 2

– Know and Trust Your People –

Ever worked for that one boss who believes that they are the *only one* who can make a decision? Or have a good idea? Or be right?

And don't they annoy the crap out of you? I mean, they really annoy you! You sit there wondering, "why in the hell did you employ me if you don't think I can do the job you employed me to do?" True!?!

Such bosses are failures! Literally. They are failures because they can never accept that, maybe, this person they employed knows more about the job they were employed to do then the person who employed them in the first place.

They're scared to seen as weak; not the embodiment of the all-conquering hero of a leader they think they should be. I have a message for any such leader, you are not a hero, you ARE weak!

You are weak because of your fear. You are weak because your fear causes you to keep other people down. You are weak because you can never put your trust in others. You are weak because it's more important for you to protect your own hide then to challenge others to greatness.

You will never be a hero, because heroes are those that sacrifice themselves for others, not for their own self-glory.

You want to be an outstanding entrepreneurial leader? Then get to know your people, trust them to do the job you engaged them to do and inspire them to be the best they can be.

Get out of their way and support them in discover a better how to.

Set aside your ego and make others great. Trust them.

And watch what happens.

"Never tell people how to do things. Tell them what to do and they will surprise you with their ingenuity"

General George Patton
1885 – 1945
General, United States Army

Commanded the U.S. Seventh Army in the Mediterranean and the U.S. Third Army in Europe during WWII. At times a controversial figure politically, he was generally admired by his troops for his aggressive style of 'go forward' leadership. Having survived the war, he died in December 1945, as a result of injuries from a motor vehicle accident.

Getting to know your people, those who work directly with you and those who contract to you or who are integral in delivering on your promises to your customers, is a key to any entrepreneur's success.

In getting to know my people, and those that supported them, I gained an understanding of their strengths, their weaknesses, what drove or demotivated them. I knew what was happening both inside and outside of their work life. They were that important to me.

Every successful entrepreneur knows that their business success comes on the back of the people they have worked with and the people they have helped; on the networks they have developed and on the relationships they have cultivated while on their journey to that success.

My billion-dollar success came on the back of the efforts of a team of people who made me look good. They knew more about what they had to do then I did. My role was to lead them, not do their job. And I found the very best – and trusted them, totally.

Did that mean I didn't know what was going on? No. I knew exactly what had to be done and exactly what had to be achieved – and watched it, closely – and got out of their way. I tracked all aspects of the business. I performed the role a leader is supposed to – ensuring that all was in place for them to do their job.

On any one day I could tell you exactly where, results wise, we were, for that day, that week, that month, that year. That's your responsibility.

If you don't know what's going on in your business to that extent, then you risk losing control of the success of your business.

"Power isn't control at all--power is strength; and giving that strength to others. A leader isn't someone who forces others to make him stronger; a leader is someone willing to give his strength to others that they may have the strength to stand on their own"

Beth Revis

1981 – current

American fantasy and science fiction author

Beth Revis is best known for the Across the Universe trilogy: *Across the Universe*, *A Million Suns* and *Shades of Earth* and her three books on writing and publishing: *Some Writing Advice*, *Some Publishing Advice* and *Some Marketing Advice*.

When I first took on my new role, before I'd even met my team, I was "counselled" by a senior manager on what he saw as a negative attribute of one of my new team members. This team member had been with the company for some months and the manager didn't like his customer service process. He asked me to correct him and bring him into line with how the manager expected him to do things.

A few years later, as I was leaving the bank, that manager questioned why I never corrected that behaviour. Frankly, I would have been stupidly crazy to do so. After watching him in action, and on seeing his results, at the time number two salesperson, and soon to be number one, in the company; I decided that, even though the approach is not one I would have used, it was in fact far more efficient and far more effective than anything my manager or I could ever have suggested. So, I let him be. Twelve years on, he is still Number One in sales.

Entrepreneurs recognise talent. But they are also willing to develop that talent where required. It has never bothered me to ever have anyone on my team more qualified than me. Equally, it has never bothered me to help someone become so good at what they do that they take their talent and go elsewhere.

My role, as a leader, is to create an environment where they could leave, but would never want to. Talent development is nothing to be feared; it is something that should be embraced.

And, if your people do leave, even going out in opposition to you – great. Celebrate with them. Because when they do, they are taking a part of you with them, the example you set of what being an entrepreneurial leader is.

The question is, what example will you set?

"Do not follow where the path may lead. Go instead where there is no path and leave a trail"

Harold R. McAlindon
1940 – 2003
Peruvian-born Professor and Author

Harold McAlindon is best known for his book, *The Little Book of Big Ideas*. He was the first President of the Cambridge Philosophy institute and former Director of the Center for Health Studies. He was one of the top academic speakers in the USA.

Chapter 3

– Get Off Your Toosh –

Entrepreneurs don't work to a clock. They work to an outcome.

They don't sit around waiting for things to happen. They make it happen. They don't watch as others do the work. They are out there ahead of the pack, showing the way.

Doing more than those they work with; committing everything to their vision, their dream, their business success. But all the time understanding that those around them will, *at the very most*, only ever commit "nearly everything" to that same vision. Because it is your baby, not necessarily theirs. They'll tell you it's a pretty baby, but compared to their own, maybe not that pretty. That's life!

Entrepreneurial leaders know that. They understand it and they accept it.

Leaders know that the example they set will become the trigger for just how beautiful their baby will be to their followers. Give 200% effort and the followers may give 90%. Give 100% effort and they may give 75%. Give 50% and you are a dead duck just waiting for the end.

Sad. Get over it, and just accept that that's the way human nature is. You can't expect anyone to commit 100% to a dream that isn't theirs. But understand this also, if your dream isn't worth 100% effort from you, then why should it be to them?

An entrepreneurial leader is one who acts 200%, to make their dreams a reality. They do more than anyone else. They drive themselves more than anyone else. They have faith in their dream more than anyone else. And they encourage their followers that the dream may just be worth following simply because they show, by their actions, just how important it is to them. How important it is to you.

"When at some future date the high court of history sits in judgment on each of us...our success or failure...will be measured by the answers to four questions: First, were we truly men of courage...? Secondly, were we truly men of judgment...? Third, were we truly men of integrity...? Finally, were we truly men of dedication...?"

John F. Kennedy
1917 – 1963
35th President of the United States:
1961 – 1963

At times controversial, he staved off a potential nuclear war with the USSR over the Cuban Crisis. He also established the Peace Corps and supported the Civil Rights Movement. A master in selling a message of hope, he maintained an average 70% approval rating during his Presidency. He was assassinated while visiting Texas on 22nd November, 1963.

Are you a person of courage? Are you willing to do what others fear to do in order to achieve the results those others will never experience? Are you willing to fail in the cause of your greatest success?

Are you a leader of sound judgement? One who is capable of making decisions, even seemingly on the fly, that are based on fact and knowledge? Are you willing to say no to an idea that isn't right to pursue in the face of outstanding opposition?

Are you a person of integrity? Where your word is your word? Where what you say is matched by what you do? Where people can trust you to be that one person who will never let them down or, at the very least, do everything you can in that cause? Will you let your people take the glory or will you wield dominion over all things successful and cast blame on all others for failures?

One is the stamp of integrity. The other is the mark of a coward.

Are you a leader dedicated to the success of your vision and to the success of your people? Will you raise them up and make them even more successful than they are now. Will you plough the way of a path that no one has ever trod before? Will your legacy be that of being remembered as a great leader, a world-changer or will your legacy be one of shame and destruction?

How you act now, in the tough times of establishing your business, sets the tone for the future of your business. The standards you set, the treatment you give, the patience and dedication you show, the vast seeping craziness of your ideas and encouragement to bring others along with you, are what will make you one to be revered or one to be reviled. It's your choice to make.

Choose wisely.

"Wisdom equals knowledge plus courage. You have to not only know what to do and when to do it, but you have to also be brave enough to follow through"

Jarod Kintz
1982 – current
Author and Humourist

Jarod Kintz has self-published over 50 books, primarily of observations and provocative quotes on politics, life, love and the future. His books include: *e-Mails from a Madman* and *Six Foot & Some Change: A Chronicle* and *Dear Natalie*.

People often assume that an entrepreneurial leader is rash, prone to jumping to conclusions and making decisions on the fly in a seemingly random response to what happens.

The truth is that the ultra-successful entrepreneur, one worthy of being a Billion-Dollar Leader, only appears that way. In truth, successful entrepreneurs spend a lot of their time gathering information, seeking opinion, watching trends and world-events. They do this so that, as other people wonder what is happening, they already know what and why and are taking action to secure the best outcome they can.

They will often act well before others even see a crisis or discover an opportunity. For this, they are often called "lucky". Lucky my derriere (I was going to put another word in here but thought better of it), they are professors of the world they operate in.

Nearly every Saturday, I will spend half a day reading every major paper I can get my hands on, reading opinion pieces from all sides of an argument. I don't just read the press whose opinions I agree with, that a self-perpetuating reinforcement of beliefs already held. I read all points of view. As Sun Tzu stated in 'The Art of War', it is an imperative to know thy enemy. You study how they act, how they think. You look at their strategic disposition, their strengths to avoid and their weaknesses to exploit. Knowing your enemy first places you in a position of strength from which to act with the greatest chance of success.

I also meet with people from all walks of business, industry and industrial relations, getting a feel for what they think, gaining insights into what actions they are taking. I track markets and trends in shares.

Entrepreneurial leaders do this, just so they can act with knowledge and act quick, while others dither. To be proactive and not reactive. To be market leaders, not market followers. To be the innovators and the disrupters. To be the great leaders that they are truly meant to be.

"Leadership is not magnetic personality, that can just as well be a glib tongue. It is not 'making friends and influencing people,' that is flattery. Leadership is lifting a person's vision to higher sights, the raising of a person's performance to a higher standard, the building of a personality beyond its normal limitations"

Peter F. Drucker
1909 – 2005
Authoritative Management Consultant & Author
Has been described as 'the founder of modern management'. He believed in lifelong learning as a path to progress and his predictions of the future of work, including his belief that the main capital of workers going forward would be in those who held knowledge, not just skills. He called them the 'knowledge worker'.

Chapter 4

– Aim High When Others Aim Low –

Every year, in every organisation I have worked with, they have set annual budgets in an attempt to come up with some magic numbers that will make the Board happy.

I have found that there are several approaches you can take in making these decisions. One, you can go over last year's figures, analyse current market trends, consult on where the market is going, obtain input from those doing the job and setting the targets based on all of that.

The second takes a bit less effort, and that is to look at the last year's figures and add 10% or so. The third takes no effort at all – pick a number, any number and then let senior management tell you what your targets will be based in their (ir)rational thinking processes. That way you can always blame 'them'!

You can figure out what process will give you a more accurate projection of the future. But, no matter what process you use to gather data, it's the next part of the decision making that determines what type of leader you are – weak or strong.

A weak leader takes that data and sets their targets based on what they think they will achieve – easily. In other words, they set base targets at a level they know they will hit. A strong leader takes that data, looks at what they know they can achieve adds a bit of stretch, or growth, to that figure and sets that as a base target. They don't set easy-to-get targets and shout out, "look what I achieved", they set harder-to-get targets and say, "look at what we achieved".

A weak leader goes for 'safe', never the impossible and so never rise to the heights reserved for those who do. Entrepreneurial leaders are never afraid to aim for the impossible on the path to greatness.

"We choose to go to the moon. We choose to go to the moon in this decade and do the other things, not because they are easy, but because they are hard, because that goal will serve to organize and measure the best of our energies and skills, because that challenge is one that we are willing to accept, one we are unwilling to postpone, and one which we intend to win, and the others, too"

John F. Kennedy
1917 – 1963
35th President of the United States:
1961 – 1963

JFK, as he was called, became the youngest person elected to the Presidency of the USA. As a Lieutenant in WWII, he and his crew survived the sinking of their boat, PT109, avoided capture and were rescued, for which he earned the Navy & Marine Corps Medal for bravery. His biography, *'Profiles in Courage'* won the Pulitzer Prize for Biography. His vision, to land Man on the moon before the end of the decade, inspired the American nation to achieve what most thought was impossible. He was assassinated before he could see that vision become a reality.

"We choose to go to the moon". Those words spoken on 12th September 1962, set a nation on the path to do what was thought impossible. On 20th July 1969, that dream was made true as Neil Armstrong declared, "That is one small step for man, one giant leap for mankind". The impossible had been made possible.

But does anyone really think that that would have become the moment in history that it became at the time it did so, without first the setting of a glorious and seemingly impossible demand? Yes, mankind may have eventually landed on the moon, at some time in the future when technology advance made running around on the moon more likely to succeed; that would have been the safe approach. Even today, with all of the advances we have made, we have still not returned to our nearest space odyssey, such is the challenge of that achievement.

Yet, in less than a decade, with technology that is dwarfed by that that is in today's mobile phone, in a spacecraft that nobody could guarantee would survive, the challenge of that call, to do that that was not easy, to do things because they were hard, was met. And the world celebrated.

Billion-Dollar Entrepreneurial leaders aim for the moon, not because it is easy, but because it is hard. Because such challenges cause us to think beyond what we currently know. They challenge us to ask a few simple questions, "What could we?" "How could we?", "What will we" and "When will we?".

What could we do to change our future? How could we do these things? Ok, so what will we do, what steps could we take to make this a reality and when will we do these things by?

But a Billion-Dollar Leader takes it one step further. They read the full text of JFK's challenge, "and the others too". Going to the moon wasn't the sole challenge issued on that day. The real challenge was everything else on which outstanding feats could be achieved. Billion-Dollar leaders know this fact, chase it and accept it as a mission to be accomplished.

"When you expect things to happen - strangely enough - they do happen"

J.P. Morgan
1837 – 1913
Financier and Banker

J.P. Morgan financed many of the major late 19th and early 20th century businesses in the USA. In 1907, his actions in securing international finance and to stabilize the price of falling stocks by actually buying those stocks, gave security to the nation, avoiding a national financial crisis. His actions during the crisis would lead to formation of the US Federal Reserve.

The reason a Billion-Dollar Entrepreneurial Leader is willing to set higher targets than most is that their expectation level for things having a successful outcome, even when difficult to achieve, is far higher than most people's.

They believe that, in saying it's possible, then there must be a way to make it possible. They know that when you find enough ways to make the impossible possible, then all you need to do is focus on making the possibles a reality. And when you make enough possibles happen then you will find that the impossible no longer that.

Leading a high-performing team means constantly believing that the impossible is possible…. somehow. You just needed to find out how.

In setting individual targets for the various teams, it was always a matter of instilling in them a belief that their targets were possible, for them, and that you believe in their ability for making the impossible happen.

In achieving the billion dollars in growth that we achieved, each of the team had to achieve targets that they had never achieved before; with each year's targets higher than the last. And each year every one of the team achieved their new targets, with some exceeding them beyond that again. Had never been done before, but they did it, year after year.

Let's put a billion dollars into perspective. Most people can probably relate to a million. A Millionaire is still considered a benchmark of being "successful" in financial terms. But a billion? If one dollar was equated to one second, it would take 11.6 days to accumulate $1,000,000. It would take 31.7 years to accumulate $1,000,000,000. We did it in three years!

You can't think ordinary when aiming so high. In achieving a billion dollars in growth, *every one of the team* had to believe more than most in the impossible. They had to act more consistently at a higher level for far longer than average people did. That's why they achieved what others didn't.

"Be fearless. Have the courage to take risks. Go where there are no guarantees. Get out of your comfort zone even if it means being uncomfortable. The road less travelled is sometimes fraught with barricades, bumps, and uncharted terrain. But it is on that road where your character is truly tested. Have the courage to accept that you're not perfect, nothing is and no one is — and that's OK"

Katie Couric

1957 – current

Journalist, TV news anchor and author

Katie Couric has been a lead news anchor on all three major American TV channels (NBC, CNN & CBS), 60 Minutes reporter, Yahoo! Global News and her own daytime talk show. In 2011 she wrote her New York Best Seller: *The Best Advice I Ever Got: Lessons from Extraordinary Lives*.

Chapter 5

- Have Faith Enough To Fail-

Rather than something to be feared, failure should be seen as a natural part of discovery. As Oprah Winfrey said, "Failure is another stepping stone to greatness". Nothing of greatness has ever happened the right way the first time. Trial and error are tied together and cannot be separated from any great success.

Steve Jobs failed. Bill Gates failed. Michael Jordan failed. Elon Musk failed. Walt Disney failed. J.K. Rowling, Steven Spielberg, Albert Einstein, Beyonce and Colonel Harland Sanders are amongst millions who have all failed on their way to achieving greatness. Yet, ultimately, we acknowledge their success. They failed, I failed and you will fail. So, acknowledge it. Prepare for it. Accept it. Celebrate it.

But, if failure is such a natural, even necessary, part of success, why then is it feared so much? Why, in so many boardrooms, in so many workplaces, in so many classrooms and fields of endeavour do those in control try to avoid failure so much?

Weak leaders fear failure because they see it as a sign of loss and not a symbol of success. They see a loss of reputation, rather than an opportunity to be heroic. They see it as a loss of control, not of strength.

Entrepreneurial leaders understand the need to fail. Because failure is a sign of progress, of eliminating that which doesn't work in order to discover what does. They know it is not about seeing failure as a proclamation to give up, but rather as a sign of hope to keep going. Our greatest glory is not in failing, but in rising every time we fail (Confucius).

Billion-Dollar Entrepreneurial Leaders are prepared to fail just as much as they are prepared to succeed.

"Don't worry about failure; you only have to be right once"

Drew Houston
1983 – current
Internet entrepreneur & co-founder/CEO of DropBox
Named as one of the most successful and influential under-30 entrepreneurs, Drew Houston is estimated to be worth over $3 billion.

It is said that, Thomas Edison failed 1,000 times before produced a long-lasting, commercially viable electrical light bulb (there are quotes that attribute this as 2,000, 7,000 and 10,000 – in this case, it's not the size that counts, it's the context in which the quote is set). Whether it was 1,000 or 10,000, Edison failed more than he succeeded. At the very best his strike rate was one in one thousand.

Can anyone list Edison's failures; even when they are probably all recorded in his journals? Do we celebrate those failures? Do we really care about those failures? The answer to all three questions is, probably not? But we do know he succeeded, once. And that's all you have to do to have history record your triumphs as an Entrepreneurial Leader.

The key was that he failed once; and got off the mat. He failed again; and had another go. Failed again and again and again and each time he got up and had another go until he found what worked. He even invented a battery for an electric car; 100 years before Elon Musk. He also held 1,093 US patents. That's a lot of failures to finding that one right thing.

Now, when people talk of Edison, they often think in singular terms – that it was just Edison himself that failed all those times. The fact is he failed a lot, just as the hundreds of workers he employed in his company failed. Because those workers were paid to fail – as they worked to discover that one magical right way of doing things. He wasn't afraid to let go and let people fail. It's their failures, as much as his, that led him to his success.

IBM built its reputation on letting people experiment on new things. So did 3M. So do many others. But not the majority; they prefer the safety of mediocrity to the risk of greatness that failure provides.

An Entrepreneurial Leader stands behind their team and defends them as they fail their way to finding that one thing right thing that works. That's why Steve Jobs was so successful and so renowned for his innovation. Be prepared to find that one thing that works by finding a thousand that don't.

"It is common sense to take a method and try it. If it fails, admit it frankly and try another. But above all, try something"

Franklin D Roosevelt
1882 – 1945
32nd President of the United States:
1933 – 1945

Considered one of the three greatest American Presidents, FDR, as he was known, served a record four terms as President; this would change in 1947 when Congress voted to limit Presidential terms to just two. His 'New Deal', a program of infrastructure development and social relief, led the US out of the Great Depression. He instigated major labour reforms and the social security system. A conservationist and environmentalist, he expanded and funded the National Parks and Forests in the US. He died in Office in April 1945.

Indecision kills. So does panic. Just ask any General in any field of war.

It was indecision that aided the failure of the ANZAC campaign in 1915, when a British General on the ground, confused about what to do, decided not to proceed to the heights of Gallipoli Cove. He failed to take the initiative, even though he knew there was no enemy in front of him; having had some of his troops actually reach the hills that would soon be the source of their defeat. Control the heights and you control the battle. Instead, he called a halt to operations, had a cup of tea and waited for orders as to what he should do. That one indecision would cost thousands of lives; fortunately, one not being my grandfather who survived.

Equally, panic is a quality that Leaders should avoid like the plague. Panic can arise as a reaction to a sudden, unexpected situation for which we are unprepared. Panic is an actual physiological response of the brain in those moments when we experience intense fear or apprehension; its aim is to keep us alive. In very simple terms, increased levels of norepinephrine and serotonin neurotransmitters activate our "fight-or-flight" response and Adrenaline is released, causing, amongst other reactions, a feeling of panic. The amygdala, a part of the brain, reacts faster than we can think to fear; we bypass our 'thinking brain' with a highly-charged emotional response to the fear. In that moment we can freeze or make stupid decisions – often wrong ones.

Airlines understand how panic kills in an emergency. Which is why their pilots spend hundreds of hours practising all types of mishaps and emergencies in a simulator. They are preparing an automatic 'learned-experience' that can be engaged by the pilot so as to overcome the emotionally charged fuzzy decision making that the untrained experience.

The Entrepreneurial Leader prepares themselves for the planned unexpected. They constantly asking the question, "What if?" and more importantly, seek solutions for if the unthinkable should become a reality. They prepare themselves to make the right decisions when bad happens. The question is, how prepared are you, right now, for the unexpected?

"Some men see things as they are and say why? I dream things that never were and say why not?"

Robert F. Kennedy
1925 – 1968
64th United States Attorney General:
1961 – 1964

Brother of President John F. Kennedy, 'Bobby', as he was called, served as a US Senator from 1965 until 1968 when, like his President brother before him, he was assassinated on 6th June. He was considered an icon of American Liberalism and advocated on issues of human rights and social justice. As Attorney General, he provided President Kennedy with advice and guidance that drew America and the USSR away from the brink of nuclear war during the Cuban Crisis of 1962

Chapter 6

- Stop Thinking Like Everyone Else -

This is the story of the 'Billion Dollar Sausage'.

Consider my situation; a new business in a new market filled with already dominant brand names. Very little, if any, brand awareness in the public at large. No money for TV, radio or print media advertising. First year target, over $200,000,000. I have 8 months. The immediate question I was faced with was this, "how do I make it happen and happen quickly". Traditional methods were out. No budget and too little time. Besides, our 'enemy' had more money and more clout to fight us should we go traditional. So, we couldn't think like they thought. We couldn't act like they would act. We had to be different – radical even.

I decided we had several advantages. We were unknown; they wouldn't take us seriously. We offered lower-cost, higher-return products. And we were owned by our members, even though most of them didn't know it, and our profits went back to them in one way or another. My major advantage though was that I had two team members who have been operating from their home offices for a short time. A third had joined just before we opened. Their knowledge and my non-conformity would form the catalyst of our success. Together, we looked for 'out there' ideas.

Our solution? Go to the workplaces of our members and do something no other bank had done – bar-b-ques. And so, a simple sausage on a piece of bread became the backbone, initially, of our success. Hundreds of sausages were cooked by the team at workplaces across the city and for those few minutes we gained the opportunity to sell the world on what we could offer. With a team willing to say, despite misgivings, 'why not?', our crazy idea worked. Those sausages made us a billion-dollars. As I've said, trust your people, know thy enemy, aim high and have enough faith.

Entrepreneurial leaders can never think like anyone else.

"A leader is one who sees more than others see, who sees farther than others see, and who sees before others see"

LeRoy Eimes
1925 – 2004
Author

Served 50 years with The Navigators and wrote 14 books including: *The Lost Art of Disciplemaking* and *Be The Leader You Were Meant To Be*.

I don't think anyone could deny that Steve Jobs was a visionary who could see things no-one else could envision. The ultimate proof of that was when Apple, the company he had formed and whose board would later dismiss him (once Apple became successful mind you), would be forced to bring him back once they recognised that it was his vision that made the difference. He could see what others couldn't.

Elon Musk and Richard Branson are definitely two modern-day visionaries who see beyond the normal sight of others. Not satisfied with things here on earth, they planned years ago to take us back to space – back to the moon and even Mars, so 'crazy' their thinking.

The world has always progressed on the back of those whose vision looked to the future – and, equally, it has been led backwards by those whose vision is stuck only on the here-and-now or, even worse, the past.

Those Leaders who see what could be build to the future. Those who lack vision strive to keep us in the past.

Progress, change, growth and opportunity only ever arise from visions of what could be. That's why an Entrepreneurial Leader has to be a forward-thinking visionary. To see what others don't. To think like others won't.

That doesn't mean that every idea works. Far from it. But by having the courage to act and the courage to fail and the courage to get up one more time and to work towards finding that one right answer, is what distinguishes an ordinary leader from an Entrepreneurial Leader.

A leader can take their people on a journey that is built around knowns. They will succeed in making their organisational goals through inspiration and those characteristics that define a good leader.

But an Entrepreneurial Leader is a step beyond. Because an Entrepreneurial Leader sees beyond the possible into a world others can't quite grasp. They gain strength from that vision. And they follow it.

"Consensus: The process of abandoning all beliefs, principles, values, and policies in search of something in which no one believes, but to which no one objects; the process of avoiding the very issues that have to be solved, merely because you cannot get agreement on the way ahead. What great cause would have been fought and won under the banner: 'I stand for consensus?'"

Baroness Margaret Thatcher
1925 – 2013
Prime Minister of United Kingdom:
1979 – 1990

Considered very much as a Stateswoman on the world scene and nicknamed 'Iron Lady' because of her uncompromising leadership style and politics, Margaret Thatcher was Britain's first female Prime Minister. She introduced major economic reforms, nicknamed 'Thatcherism', and was Prime Minister during the Falkland's War in 1982. She survived an assassination attempt in 1984 and is considered one of the great leaders of the 20th Century.

For much of my business life I have had those few trusted souls who give guidance to my decisions; these are my mentors. I have also been guided by my coaches, those independent of my business that are paid for their knowledge and input. And then there were my teams, the people I employed or worked alongside, whose operational knowledge and ideas of how things might work guided me in my decision making. Those were the people I choose to listen to.

And these are the types of people you would be wise to listen to also.

But, while the input of those you trust is important, there were times where you will be asked to stand alone in your decisions. Even if those decisions are against what many say you should or shouldn't do.

But, beware. Such decisions come with a double-edged sword. With such decisions comes the very personal responsibility you will hold for the consequences those decisions may deliver. Blame will not be to others.

But that doesn't mean you should shy away from making unpopular or hard decisions – you just have to be well prepared for making them and knowledgeable enough to know why you should be making them in the face of such opposition.

That's the burden of leadership. Your "the buck stops here!" moment.

Consensus may make life easier, but it may not lead to success. Because consensus may be reached with people who cannot see the way forward as you do. They may not hold the vision as you do. They may not have all the knowledge and awareness of well thought-out risk solutions as you do. They may not be willing to take those risks or to change like you are willing to do. Such consensus kills ideas and limits possibilities.

It may not be easy, but an Entrepreneurial Leader is willing to make the call on such decisions. To take the calculated risk. And to accept the responsibility, while planning solutions, should things not go as planned.

"It is not the critic who counts. The credit belongs to the man who is actually in the arena, whose face is marred by dust & sweat & blood; who strives valiantly; who errs, who comes short again & again, because there is no effort without error and shortcoming; but who does actually strive to do the deeds; who knows great enthusiasms, the great devotions; who spends himself in a worthy cause; who at the best knows in the end the triumph of high achievement, & who at the worst, if he fails, at least fails while daring greatly, so that his place shall never be with those cold & timid souls who neither know victory nor defeat"

Theodore Roosevelt
1858 – 1919
26th President of the United States:
1901 – 1909

Nicknamed 'The Rough Rider', a title earned as a Colonel in the US Cavalry during the Spanish-American war of 1898. A lifelong naturalist, he established many of America's national parks and forests. His face appears next to those of Lincoln, Washington and Jefferson on the Mount Rushmore monument. In 1906 he won the Nobel Peace Prize for brokering the end of the Russo-Japanese War. One of his lasting legacies is the construction of the Panama Canal.

Chapter 7

- Celebrate and Reward! -

As the last century was rushing to close, I was tasked with changing the way a business did business. Over 12 months in one city and another 15 months in an overseas location, I conducted a program that would change the way service was delivered and how team members were recognised for their success. And a major key to the success of those transformational programs was a simple chocolate frog.

Long story short, every employee from the GM down was involved in deciding how, in their role, they could deliver on the promises that our organisation's values and mission made. Service standards and the way things were done were set, not by management, but by each of the team members themselves. They figured out how they would deliver on excellence.

Every month, each team member, again from the GM down, had two individual targets and one team target upon which they would be measured, each based on the standards they had set in their team. Importantly, the individual targets were just that. They were set based on what that one person decided would be their focus of improvement in delivering excellence that month. Not a punishment measure, these were development plans put in action.

But such actions needed to be rewarded, otherwise it would become a punishment – a look at what you didn't do rather than at what you did. And so the chocolate frog. One target, one frog. Nine frogs in three months, a shopping voucher. Another three months, an even bigger voucher. More again, the possibility of an overseas trip to a major event. A simple frog lead to a major reward. What they achieved was recognised.

An Entrepreneurial Leader ensures individual achievements are both publicly recognised and rewarded. The return is loyalty and success.

"Before you are a leader, success is all about growing yourself. When you become a leader, success is all about growing others"

Jack Welch
1935 – current
CEO, Chairman, Author and Engineer

As Chairman and CEO or General Electric (1981 – 2001) he led the organisation to realise a 4,000% increase in the value of the company. He introduced the concept of the 'boundaryless company', with an emphasis on finding great ideas from within the company. He is author of: *What Makes A Leader* and *Winning* and *Jack: Straight From The Gut*.

I think the greatest pleasure I get from all the years of business development I have been a part of, is seeing the growth and providing the opportunity for growth in the people I have worked with.

One huge mistake any leader can make is to believe that they are indispensable. Try this trick. Fill a glass with water. Now, put one finger in the water. The water has given space for your finger to be in it. It's there, just like the role you perform in your work is there. It's quite visible for everyone to see. Now, take your finger out of the water. What happens to the space your finger created? It fills with water; it's as if your finger had never been there. In time, as people move on, nobody will recall a finger ever being there anyway. And if a finger is ever needed in the water at some time in the future, then it will be a different one. Similar, but not the same as yours. It's the same in the role we perform in our work.

In the airforce, we used to say that someone would be promoted to their level of incompetence. After that, you should have some really smart people surrounding you. A real leader understands that it is the people around them, the people who do the hundreds of every-day tasks required to make a business successful, that are vital to their success as a leader. They also understand that in order to avoid becoming redundant, they need to develop the people below them who can take their place.

To progress in any organisation, those above you need to feel confident that the work you are responsible for can still be done once you are promoted. Otherwise they will leave you where you are and find someone to take that place above you.

Never be afraid to develop your people. Give them opportunity to grow and become better at what they do. Let them gain new skills, new ideas and even new career pathways. Let them learn how to be a great leader in their own right. Teach them all they need to know to replace you in order that you can move on new opportunities yourself.

An Entrepreneurial Leader knows the importance of developing others.

"Success is the doing, not the getting; in the trying, not the triumph. Success is a personal standard, reaching for the highest that is in us, becoming all that we can be. If we do our best, we are a success"

Zig Ziglar

1926 – 2012

Author, Motivational Speaker Salesman

Zig Ziglar was one of the greatest and most sought-after speakers of the late 20th Century. He was one of the must-see speakers, along with such greats as Dr Norman Vincent Peale, Cavett Robert and Bill Gove. His first book, *See You At The Top*, led to his catchcry speech finish, "I'll see you, and I mean you, at the top". Published in 1975, it is still a top seller. His final book *Born To Win: Find Your Success Code*, was published in 2012. His are still must read books.

The standards you set for yourself will become the standards by which all others measure themselves. The values and ethics you display in your role as a leader will become the values and ethics delivered by those who look upon you as their leader.

Why would you expect anything else? You can't! Followers will always mimic their leader. If you expect excellence in service, deliver excellence yourself. If you require a creative workplace, be creative and reward creativity yourself. If you expect trust, loyalty, compassion, currency of knowledge, ongoing education and continuous personal improvement then lead by the example you set in all of those.

It is the values of the leader that will determine their value as a leader.

A Billion-Dollar Entrepreneurial Leader is not one who sits back and waits for things to happen. They are there on the front foot making it happen. They work to continuously improve and to be more knowledgeable this day then they were the day before. They know they cannot accept complacency in their quest to always be one step ahead of the opposition.

A leader who believes that they have all the knowledge they will ever need to be an ongoing success is a fool. What you know today will be redundant tomorrow. Just look at the way technology and its effect on the way we do business has changed in the past five years, let alone ten. And yet, I know of managers who still refuse to adapt to this new way of business, instead, spending every day whinging about how that technology is taking customers away from them. They blame rather than adapt.

Entrepreneurial Leaders know it's important to understand what is happening in the business, social and political worlds, not just locally, but globally. They accept that they must put themselves on a path of continuous learning and improvement. They strive to always be the very best they can be in order to achieve the type of success others aren't willing to pay the price for.

"You are not here merely to make a living. You are here in order to enable the world to live more amply, with greater vision, with a finer spirit of hope and achievement. You are here to enrich the world, and you impoverish yourself if you forget the errand"

Woodrow Wilson
1856 – 1924
28th President of the United States:
1913 to 1921

Woodrow Wilson led the United States during WWI. In 1919 he was one of the founding leaders of the League of Nations, the organisation that would eventually become the United Nations.

Chapter 8

- Move On, Move Out, Start Over -

I have come to believe that truly great leaders are rare. Those are the leaders who give rise to a vision that affects the world in a significantly pronounced way, who make a difference on a global scale and whose name will be forever etched in the annals of the world's history.

But I also believe that there are many, many great leaders who will leave their mark on their society, on their country, within their circle of influence, even on the worldwide theatre; not to the same extent as those truly great ones, but in their own way of greatness.

Each are equally important in making this world a better place. Thousands of smaller cumulative changes can have just as significant role collectively over time as one major change on its own. We notice the significant change for what it is, totally disruptive, and somehow absorb the myriad of smaller changes happening all around us, seemingly without noticing.

Equally, I believe that there are leaders who are best at starting up an enterprise and there are those leaders who are better running an established organisation. I believe that entrepreneurial leaders, the ones who spend their time and energy getting an enterprise of the ground, who push the limits to drive through change and display tenacity in making things happen, love all of that – but become bored running the day-to-day operations, with only the occasional disruptive change event to excite them. They hate being baby sitters. Whereas, the not-so-entrepreneurial leader, the steady-hand-at-the-tiller leader is perfectly suited, in temperament, to this scenario. Both are valid leaders. Both are needed.

It's important that an Entrepreneurial Leader knows why, plans for and has a strategy already in place, for when they will move on from their baby. It may be a new role or a totally new business. Just be prepared.

"Find out who you are and be that person. That's what your soul was put on this Earth to be. Find that truth, live that truth and everything else will come"

Ellen DeGeneres
1958 – current
TV Talk-show Host, Comedian Actress

Between 1994 and 2002, Ellen DeGeneres starred in her own sitcoms, *Ellen* & *The Ellen Show* before becoming the host of her long-running talk show, *The Ellen DeGeneres Show*, in 2003. She has long been an LGBT activist and has won many awards for her activist and charity works. In 2016, she received the *Presidential Medal of Freedom*, the highest civilian award in the United States.

"You can't be anyone else but you Colin, so stop trying to be them and just be you." I've cut out the expletives that accompanied that rest of that telling off by my coach. He'd just given me a lesson I had to learn. For years I'd measured my success based on the success of others. I'd tried to mould myself into being "just like them"; I'm not alone in that.

It was only when I came to terms with who I was, the type of person I wanted to be in order to be the very best me I could be and the things in life that were important to me, only then could I truly be me. Only then could I make my mark as only I could. Similar to, not same as.

In finding out who I truly was, I discovered my strengths, my weaknesses. I discovered what I liked doing and what I never wanted to do again. I acknowledged what I was good at and how I could focus those talents and it is this that led me to doing the things in business that I have done.

It also lets me acknowledge the limits of the things I either can't do or could do; but choose not to. This allows me to take the positive step of surrounding myself with those who can do those things. That has to be far better than thinking I can do everything and stuffing everything up, which I've seen some managers do so badly. It is so easy to get caught up in one's own hype, especially when surrounded by those who only ever tell you what you want to hear.

Which is why my coaches are so important to me. They tell me what I need to hear. That honesty at times sucks. It hurts. But when I evaluate what they have said against what I want to achieve, then I am able to make a decision, one way or another, on how I will be the very best person, the very best citizen, the very best leader I can be.

A Billion-Dollar leader works at being the very best they can be. They seek the truth and define exactly what it is that makes them who they are and exactly what it is that they need to do to be that. They define the values they will display. The set the limits they want set. In truth they find strength, not weakness; an honest, status building integrity. Be the truth!

"Your playing small does not serve the world... as we let our own light shine, we unconsciously give other people permission to do the same.... and as we are liberated from our own fear, we automatically liberate others"

Nelson Mandela
1918 – 2013
President of South Africa:
1994 – 1999

Nelson Mandela was an internationally recognised anti-apartheid activist, philanthropist and political leader. He was born into the Thembu royal family and became a lawyer before joining the African National Congress (ANC) in 1943. In 1962 he was arrested for conspiring to overthrow the state and was imprisoned. Even from prison he would affect the history of South Africa and in 1990, he was released by the South African President, F.W. de Klerk, who feared a racial war. In 1994, both men negotiated an end to apartheid and the first multiracial elections were held, ending in Nelson Mandela being elected as President. His story is told in his book: *Long Walk To Freedom*.

To whom much is given, much is expected. Ancient words, and wise ones.

Being a Billion-Dollar Entrepreneurial Leader is about more than just you being successful. It is more than the adulation, the sacrifice and the rewards that your success will bring you and those you love and care for.

Everything you do as an entrepreneur, every vision you hold as a leader who thinks bigger than others think, who sees more than others see, every action you take and every decision you make is bigger than just you.

Nobody on this planet has been given that vision just as you have. Similar maybe, not same.

Nobody on this planet has been given the talent that you have to make that vision a reality, Similar maybe, not same.

Your vision is unique to you. Just as you are unique to you. There is no-one on earth the same as you.

Which means that nobody can do what you are meant to do – to bring your vision to life. To give to this world the idea that you have been given. It is yours for a reason. Nobody else but you can do it.

To dismiss your idea, to not take action, to not gather around you those who can help you make it all happen, to limit your thinking to the possible and not the impossible, to not make people better than they were and to reward them for what they have done, to not become the very best you that you are meant to be, to give up when you could have gone on to even greater things, to not believe in yourself when others do and to not make your vision a reality – is to rob this world of something great.

And, in the words of Nelson Mandela – a truly great leader – when we set our vision free, when we step up to make the impossible possible, when we show the integrity of belief in action, when we show what's possible, then we shine a light that let's others know that their dream is possible too. Be a light to the future. Liberate their belief that anything is possible.

About The Author: Colin Emerson

MBA : Graduate Certificate Management : Diploma of Teaching(TAFE)

Colin Emerson has built a reputation as a successful Leadership & Organisational Development Strategist & Coach. For more than 20 years Colin has conducted leader and leadership development programmes for local and international companies and major universities. Colin is also author of *"The Values Inspired Leader'*, which discusses the values required to lead yourself and your team in today's world.

He has delivered over 1,000 seminars, speaking engagements and workshops for leading corporations, training institutions, Universities and government agencies in Australia, New Zealand and USA.

"A few years ago, I discovered what it takes to bring together a group of people who could build a brand-new business by a billion dollars in only 3 years in a market already dominated by 5 nationally-branded competitors. Basically we whipped their tails. So, as they say in the classics, been there, done that. These days though, I use that knowledge; I use my leadership and business building experiences to help entrepreneurs & leaders, people just like you, become Billion Dollar Leaders in their own right. To become the leader, the entrepreneur and the brand that others aspire to be"